REL IGION
vs.
ATIONSHIP

Are you religious? Don't answer that yet!

Gary Simons with Belle Simons

Religion vs. Relationship Life Application Devotional

Library of Congress Cataloging-in-Publication Data
Gary Simons with Belle Simons 2021
Religion vs. Relationship Life Application Devotional
p. cm.
ISBN 9798545780761

English Version: Unless otherwise indicated, all Scripture quotations are taken from the New International Version.® Copyright © 1973, 1978, 1984, 2011 by the International Bible Society.

2021 First Edition

Printed in Columbia, South Carolina, United States of America

Available in English and Mandarin Chinese
中文、英文版本

Dedication

We dedicate this devotional to our children:
Aiden
Jasmine
Arian

We constantly pray that God will lead you into a genuine,
abundant relationship with Him to impact your
generation and those who
will come behind you.

Acknowledgements

I am truly grateful for Shaun Bailey, Vernette Sukdeo and
Eric Woods for their countless
hours of editing. And very special thanks
to my extraordinary wife and co-author,
Belle, for her incredible insight, sound
wisdom, and faithful support she
constantly gives to this
ordinary man.

CONTENTS

INTRODUCTION

ARE YOU RELIGIOUS? DON'T ANSWER THAT YET!

The concept of writing a devotional came out of the vision of discipleship at GracePoint, a non-denominational church. Part of our core mission is to teach people to follow Jesus as we grow in God's grace. We accomplish this starting from the biblical yet practical teaching of our Sunday series. The application from the Sunday message is then discussed in our small groups each week. It was then decided that a life application devotional would help ensure we apply what we've already been taught. This 3-fold step of discipleship would ultimately lead to a deeper relationship with Christ.

Most believers would not classify themselves as religious. After all, many understand that to believe in Jesus as personal Savior means that you embark on a unique "relationship" with Christ. However, to hold to the assumption that you're on the right spiritual track and not religious in any way is to nullify the opportunity for God to show you otherwise. So let's open our minds and hearts as we allow God to lead us on our spiritual journey together.

You may be surprised by what you'll discover within your spiritual walk as you progress through this devotional. You're almost guaranteed to discover existing mindsets and actions which may put you in the religious category. The truth is, we can quickly adopt a religious mindset and lifestyle, just like the religious people in the Bible.

These religious bent teachers knew the Bible inside-out, but were far from having a heart for God. They had a greater commitment to their own manufactured rules than following the words of Jesus. In fact, with all of their knowledge of the Bible in their heads, they still cried out "crucify Him" from their hearts. The ones who were supposed to help people see the Messiah were the ones who were blind to His life and mission. If we're not careful, we can become just like them.

The purpose of this devotional is to explore how we can avoid having a religious mindset regarding our relationship with God. To understand how to build a godly relationship, we need to explore the truth from two angles. The first is we need to reveal the most common mindsets religious people have. We do this not to follow their example but to learn what not to do. The second is to expound on what we need to do to build a relationship. This devotional will explore both. I hope that you will break through to the life-giving relationship with God that Jesus offers to all who believe in Him. No matter where you are on your spiritual journey, it's good to know that at every turn, Jesus is inviting you to depart from the mundane rut of being a religious person to enter a joyful and vibrant relationship with Him.

BEFORE YOU GET STARTED

Pray and ask God to open your mind and heart to what He will have you change in your life. May God lead you to a closer relationship with Him.

WEEK 1

GETTING STARTED

ĐAY 1: RECALCULATING

I recall one weekend when my wife, Belle, and I, along with her family, decided to visit a tea garden in the mountains of central Taiwan. The region is called Nantou, which is known for exporting its high mountain tea. It is a remote area, so we had to rely on Google Maps to get us there as we departed from the city in the mid-morning. During our estimated 6-hour journey, we stumbled across various quaint shops and eateries along the way. We were careful to follow every turn directed by the GPS on my phone. Over the mountains, through the towns, pass the rice fields we went.

At sunset, I glanced at the time remaining before our arrival, and I discovered that we weren't going to reach our destination until well into the night. Within the last hour of following Google Maps, the terrain was getting more and more challenging. From the main road to the off-beaten sand trails and secluded gardens, we finally heard, "You have arrived," only to discover as we were able to look more carefully that we were near the edge of a cliff in the middle of nowhere!

Google Maps misled us! We thought we had arrived at our destination, but after a phone call, we discovered we were still 30 minutes away. The same thing can happen to us spiritually as we consider religion versus relationship. As we follow "our" GPS and not God's, we may think we're right on track with where God wants us to be, which is a thriving relationship with Christ.

However, with additional observation, we may discover that we're further down the off-beaten path of religion than we had ever anticipated. Therefore, spiritual recalculation is required to get to the place where we should be. This is what the Religion versus Relationship devotional is all about. It's taking the time to recalculate the areas of our lives where we may be off track to get back on the road where God wants us to be.

The foremost essential you must pack on this trip is a sufficient dose of humility. It takes humility to admit that we're wrong and need redirection. It takes a humble heart to call on God for help and to submit to the promptings of the Holy Spirit. Why is this essential so important? Because the God we serve is magnetically attracted to your humility. That is the only way you will be able to enjoy the grace of God. In His gentleness, He not only tells us where we're wrong but He's faithful to lead us back to the destination of relationship.

TODAY'S WORD
James 4:6 NKJV
But He gives more grace. Therefore He says: "God resists the proud, but gives grace to the humble."

WHAT DOES IT MEAN?

To maintain a close relationship with God, you will need to spiritually position yourself in a way to receive God's grace constantly. God's grace is defined as the unmerited favor God gives you to live for Him that you don't deserve. Just because we can quote the Bible or say "God bless you" and recite religious terms doesn't mean we have fulfilled Jesus' teachings for fostering a genuine relationship with God by His grace.

James, the half-brother of Jesus, makes it clear that God resists the proud. Pride is the fuel that feeds a religious mindset. Pride shows up in performance for acceptance, service for praise, and acts of kindness for recognition. The moment people become the greater audience than God it leads one on the path of becoming religious. Jesus was abundantly clear about how he felt about religion. He did not hold back any words regarding his dissatisfaction with people who claim to be "holy" but have no heart for God.

WHAT DOES IT MATTER?

Inviting the grace of God in our lives is required to experience more of the power of God. It is the key to developing a vibrant relationship with Christ. Self-sufficiency suffocates grace. It short-changes the life of Christ for self, leading one to become a discouraged, defeated, and a distressed Christian. It is grace that keeps your relationship with Christ vibrant. However, the foundational flaw of religion is to be deceived into thinking you need to live *for* Jesus and be independent. Yet, the foundational framework required of relationship is to stop living *for* Jesus and allow the life of Christ to live **through** you, knowing that you need to be dependent.

As night differs from day, so religion differs from relationship. An unknown author described it this way. "Religion is someone in church thinking about fishing; relationship is someone out fishing thinking about God." So replace "fishing" with your favorite hobby, whether it's golfing, shopping, or the spa.

To love someone means they'll continuously be on your mind and heart. Jesus wants that type of relationship with you. He wants to be the overriding focus of your whole heart. So as we advance through this devotional, let's listen out for God's confirming words, "You have arrived." Let's arrive together to abundance, to a growing and close relationship with Him.

BEFORE YOU GO
Before you go on to your next task, take a few minutes to pray and ask God to speak to you and show what mindsets and attitudes need to change to go deeper in your relationship with Christ.

The magnet to God's grace is humility, and its power is released by dependency.

ᗪᎯY 2: ᒪᎬᎢ'Ꮪ ᗪᎬFIᑎᎬ IᎢ

Both Christians and non-believers can fall into the danger of being religious. The danger is two-fold. For the unbeliever, it can provide a false sense of security regarding salvation. This results in a false sense of safety concerning their eternal state and will result in the words of Jesus, *"... 'I never knew you. Away from me, you evildoers!'" Matthew 7:23b.*

On the other hand, being religious is dangerous for the believer because the abundant life is replaced with a life bound by rules that the Spirit of God cannot empower. To demonstrate the prevalence of being religious, let's look at a survey by the Barna Group. Over one-third of people in the United States identify themselves as Christians but do not believe the Holy Spirit is real. Overall, 38% strongly agreed, and 20% agreed somewhat that the Holy Spirit is "a symbol of God's power or presence, but is not a living entity."[1] I won't be surprised if these statistics were similar in other countries as well.

If the Holy Spirit is not real, how can we be saved? The Apostle Paul made it clear that the Holy Spirit is a person in the God-head, and without the Spirit, we don't have Christ.
"...And if anyone does not have the Spirit of Christ, they do not belong to Christ." Romans 8:9b.
These statistics demonstrate that many claim to know Christ but deny His power. The Holy Spirit is

the One who gives us the power to carry out the will of God.

TODAY'S WORD
2 Timothy 3:5 (NLT)
They will act religious, but they will reject the power that could make them godly. Stay away from people like that!

WHAT DOES IT MEAN?
Many spiritual people enjoy the comfort zone of being religious on the outside but lack genuine transformation from the inside. Paul tells Timothy to beware of the influence of such people on your Christian life.

To appreciate the danger of being religious, we need to define it. A person can be religious in one of four ways.

Definition 1:
You're religious when you take confidence in your righteousness rather than the righteousness of Jesus Christ. This refers to those who have not accepted Jesus as personal Savior. They don't accept that salvation is by grace through faith. Instead, they rely on their good works to save them. The Bible speaks clearly against this approach to salvation in *Ephesians 2:8-9,*
8"For it is by grace you have been saved, through faith - and this is not from yourselves, it is the gift of God- 9 not by works, so that no one can boast."

The remaining three definitions are so deceptive because they can easily sneak even into the lives of believers.

Definition 2:
 You are religious when you attempt to worship God by following a system of man-made rules as if those rules are equal to the Bible.

Definition 3:
You are religious when you obey God to be accepted by Him, rather than obey God because you're already accepted.

Definition 4:
 You are religious when you can forgive yourself for your shortcomings but can't offer love and forgiveness to others who fall short.

All four of the above definitions originate from the trinity of self-righteousness consisting of 'me, myself, and I.' Being religious is incredibly deceptive because it's a pattern of living that is least recognized by the person operating in it.

WHAT DOES IT MATTER?
Righteousness, however, is found in Jesus Christ, and He freely credits His righteousness to the one who believes. Jesus, who had no sin, died for our sins on the cross, was buried, and rose again on the third day. Therefore, anyone who admits they've sinned and believes in Jesus is given the righteousness of God through Christ.

2 Corinthians 5:21
God made him who had no sin to be sin for us, so that in him we might become the righteousness of God.

To have the righteousness of Christ is to be fully accepted by God. However, self-righteousness is when we strive to be accepted by God by what we do, instead of resting in the righteousness of Jesus Christ based on what He has done.

Before we go further, let's pause to ensure we have accepted Jesus Christ as personal Savior. Then, take some time to reflect on whether you have truly accepted Christ. If you haven't, make sure today by praying to God by admitting that you have sinned and believe that Jesus died and rose again for you.

Here is a prayer of salvation that you can pray in faith to God:

> *Dear God,*
> *I admit that I have sinned against You. And I believe that You sent Jesus to live a perfect life and die on the cross for my sins. Jesus, I believe that You shed Your blood for me, and I believe that You were buried and rose again on the third day. I confess that You are my Lord.*
> *Jesus, please come into my life and save me right now.*

Thank you for dying for me, and I thank
You that one day I shall see You face to face.
In Jesus' name, Amen.

BEFORE YOU GO

If you've been a believer for many years, a few months, or just accepted Christ today, God has a plan for you. So pray right now and ask God to speak to you about any area where you may be leaning on religion more than a real relationship with Christ.

Tomorrow we'll talk more about the definition of religion as we discuss the essential understanding of spiritual acceptance. See you then.

The law condemns the best of us;
but grace saves the worst of us.
~Joseph Prince

DAY 3: IN THE RIGHT ORDER

My nephew decided to take on the brave adventure of being an aviation pilot. In his determination, he went to SunState Aviation at Kissimmee, Florida, and underwent an intensive training program to become a private pilot.

After he mastered flying with a co-pilot, he eventually graduated to flying solo and was later able to take passengers. This time, instead of flying over Florida, it was now the beautiful Island of Bermuda. He invited me to join him on a flight. Now, this was something that I had never experienced. It was exhilarating to look at Bermuda for about an hour from an ariel view of a small airplane.

However, one thing I noticed before we were airborne. He had to undergo a rigorous checklist which consisted of a specific order from prechecks to take-off. Without this order, getting airborne would have been impossible. The same is true when it comes to works and acceptance. When placed in the correct order, the freedom from a relationship with Jesus will take off. However, when it's reversed, you'll be continually grounded by the weight of religion. The reversed order prevents you from obtaining clearance for take-off. Let's talk about the order of works and acceptance.

TODAY'S WORD
Ephesians 2:8-10
8 For it is by grace you have been saved, through faith - and this is not from yourselves, it is the gift of God - 9 not by works, so that no one can boast. 10 For we are God's handiwork, created in Christ Jesus to do good works, which God prepared in advance for us to do.

WHAT DOES IT MEAN?
Notice the essential order here. You get saved by God's grace and faith, but once you've accepted Christ, you do good works (verse 8). It's not the good works that saves you; instead, you do the good works after you're saved. Religion places works first, then acceptance. Relationship places acceptance first, then works. Notice that after salvation, we're called God's handiwork. "Handiwork" means we are His masterpiece.

However, we cannot reach God's degree of craftmanship without doing the good works that He predestined us to fulfill. It's always salvation and acceptance first, then good works.

WHAT DOES IT MATTER?
Religion says, *"I do to be accepted."* A religious person does good works to be accepted by God. They tend to think that if they do enough good works, God will notice and accept them by granting them eternal life or right standing before Him. However, relationship says, *"I'm accepted, so I do.'* In other words, it's not good works that get

you to heaven, as many believe, but it's God's grace along with your faith that gives you the right standing before God to get you to heaven. Therefore, being heaven-bound is not based on your performance, works, or achievements. It's only found in God giving you salvation you don't deserve. The crux of religion versus relationship is how you view salvation.

At the same time, religion is so dangerous that you can slip into the rut of being a religious person even after accepting Christ. Although this does not reverse your salvation, it short-changes you from experiencing the abundant life that Jesus intended for you to live. So ensure you maintain the correct order. Salvation first, then works. It's the only way you can soar.

BEFORE YOU GO
Before you head off, remember to pray and ask God to stop you when you try to work to be accepted by God. Instead, ask Him to confirm with you that you're entirely accepted by Him, then seek to work and fulfill His will for your life.

Christianity is not a religion; it's a loving relationship like no other.
~Author Unknown

25

DAY 4: IT'S ALL ABOUT MOTIVES

Motives matter! The Bible speaks a great deal about our motives and how they should be in the right place. People who are focused on religion and those who are focused on relationship have opposing motivations.

Religious people are primarily motivated by being accepted. This could involve doing works to be accepted by God or doing good works to be accepted by others. Relationship-driven people are primarily motivated by doing good out of an expression of gratitude because God has already accepted them. Their good works are an expression of their thanks for God's love in their lives.

Today's verse is to help realign our understanding of ensuring we have the right motive when we serve God. Serving Him has to be an expression of our love for Him. We should not obey or serve God to be accepted by Him.

TODAY'S WORD
1 John 4:19
We love because he first loved us.

WHAT DOES IT MEAN?
Notice that obedience is the by-product of our love for God. However, the reason why we love God and others is that He has loved us FIRST.
God is the One who initiates the relationship.
Building a healthy relationship with God comes

with realizing that we're not trying to obtain His love by doing good works. Instead, we're demonstrating our love through our good works. Serving God is simply a response to the unconditional love that He has lavished on us. Remember what Paul said about motives. He said there would come a time when Jesus will evaluate the motive behind our good works.

1 Corinthians 3:13
their work will be shown for what it is, because the Day will bring it to light. It will be revealed with fire, and the fire will test the quality of each person's work.

WHAT DOES IT MATTER?
This verse begins with "their work." The inference is when your time on earth is done, Jesus will evaluate the works you did for Him while here. Each born-again Christian will stand individually before Jesus for their good works will be assessed on that Day. "The Day" usually refers to the Day of the Lord or the Day of God's judgment.

For the believer, this isn't designed to be a judgment to be feared. Instead, it should be considered more of a rewards celebration to look forward to if you're carefully following Jesus. The light of Christ's eyes will evaluate the motive behind our good works. If you did ministry for the glory of God rather than yourself or others, works would be fireproof. On the other hand, even the greatest acts of kindness done with an ulterior motive, such as to impress others or to "earn" God's love, will be burnt to smithereens.

Finally, notice that Paul also says that the fiery eyes of Christ will test the quality of each person's work. Of course, quantity is important to God, but that's not the single area of evaluation here. It's also the quality. Bad quality is produced when we do things for God with a wrong motive to impress others. Sound quality is produced when we do things for God to bring Him glory. Having the right motive is what rescues us from the clutches of religion.

BEFORE YOU GO
Before heading off to the next thing: If you're active in ministry, such as: helping others, singing on the worship team or choir, leading a Bible study or small group, ask God to evaluate your motives behind your good works to ensure they are an expression of your love for Him.

It's not only what you do for God that matters most, but why you do it.

DAY 5: WHO DO YOU SERVE?

The word "serve" appears over 50 times in the New Testament. Any king requires servants. The kingship of Jesus Christ is no different. He is known not only as the Messiah, which means 'Anointed One', but also as the King of kings and the Lord of lords (1 Timothy 6:15).

When we accepted Jesus Christ as personal Savior, we also became the servants of Christ. When Jesus was on earth, He left us with the ultimate example of what service is. He not only taught the concept but fleshed it out in the most potent display in history. Jesus demonstrated what servanthood is by dying on the cross for our sins. As the resurrected Lord, He now expects us to follow His example to serve Him by our love for God and others. This brings us to today's passage.

TODAY'S WORD
Colossians 3:23 NLT
Whatever you do, do it from the heart, as something done for the Lord and not for people,

WHAT DOES IT MEAN?
Why is this verse so important when it comes to the topic of religion versus relationship? We become religious when we serve people more than we serve Christ. Let me explain because this is one of the religious mindsets that can easily remain undetected in our lives. First of all, God commands us to serve one another. However, the problem

arises when we're more concerned about serving people than serving the Lord.

How do you know when you're serving people more than you're serving God when the actions appear the same? Our motive is only revealed when we're tested. For example, your motive is tested when you're serving in ministry, and someone offends you, rubs you the wrong way, or forgets to give you the credit you feel you deserve. If you decide to get an attitude and quit the ministry service you're doing, you're most likely a 'church server' rather than a 'Christ server.' You've fallen into the pothole of being a religious person.

WHAT DOES IT MATTER?

When people who serve Christ get hurt in ministry, they continue to press on because they are doing it for Jesus.

Yes, there may be a time when God moves them on, and they have to leave, but it won't be a knee-jerk reaction because someone hurt you or disrespected you. Aren't you glad that Jesus didn't quit His ministry to us when the Pharisees falsely defamed His character, or when He was ridiculed and misunderstood by His own family or insulted by the Romans? Jesus knew He was first and foremost serving God. And let's face it. When others offend you when you're trying to serve them, the human reaction is to retaliate or quit. However, when you're fully convinced that God has called you, you'll allow the offense to build you instead of break you. So, who do you serve? Christ or the church. Life has a way of revealing the truth in time.

BEFORE YOU GO

Before you continue with the next task, take some time to pray and ask the Spirit of God to evaluate your heart. Ask Him to ensure you fulfill His will and to confirm in your heart that you're serving God Himself.

Difficult times don't create discontentment,
they only expose what's already there.

DAY 6: WHO DO YOU FOLLOW?

Whenever you join the military, there is one thing that you must learn to do in Boot Camp. You must learn to march. Undergoing marching drills is one of the primary disciplines that a new recruit must master to be an effective soldier. It demonstrates uniformity and a sense of pride, but it also teaches the vital lesson of submission. A soldier must follow the person marching in front of them based on the direction of the section's leader. The leader is the one who yells out the order of the march. There is no swerving to the right or left. There are no individual agendas when marching. It involves conformity and submission based on when and where the leader goes.

The same is true when it comes to obeying God. And the only way to truly follow God is to obey His Word. It's the Word of God that calls the shots in our own lives. Our job is to conform and submit to the Word. The problem arises when we pattern our lives more to what society or religious organizations are saying than obeying the Word of God.

The religious people of Jesus' time made a grave error. They treated manufactured rules as if they were equal to the Word of God. Eventually, this led to legalism and a judgmental spirit. We fall into the same rut of legalism when we do the same. When we allow man-made rules or even society to become a greater influence than the Word of God, we may be marching, but to the wrong beat. We are following a system that will only lead to pride and ruin. This brings us to today's passage.

TODAY'S WORD
Acts 17:11
Now the Berean Jews were of more noble character than those in Thessalonica, for they received the message with great eagerness and examined the Scriptures every day to see if what Paul said was true.

WHAT DOES IT MEAN?
Berea was a region not too far from Philippi, yet closer to Thessalonica by approximately 45 miles (73 kilometers). It was a Macedonian city that Paul visited during his second missionary journey. Before going to Berea, Paul and Silas had an eventful visit in Philippi where a Philippian jailer and his whole family had accepted Christ. They then traveled to Thessalonica, where Paul taught the Jews for three weeks, resulting in some Jews, many Greeks, and a few prominent women following Christ. However, it was because of the jealousy of the religious Jews who rounded up some people to start a riot that caused Paul and Silas to flee to the next city of Berea.

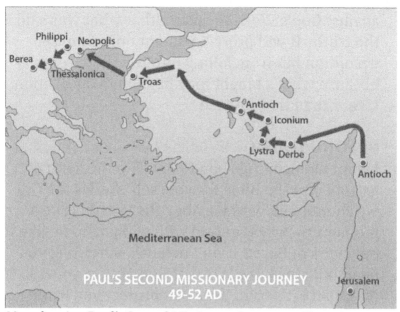

Map showing Paul's Second Missionary Journey to Berea [2]

What is so significant about this particular visit? Paul saw something in these believers that he had not seen in the previous cities. Not only did they receive his teaching, but more importantly, they went away and examined the Bible for themselves to ensure that Paul was speaking the truth.

WHAT DOES IT MATTER?

This is the missing practice within Christian circles today. Many come ready to receive the Word, but few examine the Bible after to ensure that what was said was true.

I want to encourage you from this day forward because who you follow matters most. Whenever you hear the Word of God taught, never take it at face value. Take the time to examine the teaching against God's Word to ensure that what was said is the truth. It will protect you not only from self-deception but from falling into the rut of religion because what's taught may be human fabrication rather than God-birthed.

BEFORE YOU GO

I want to encourage you to develop the habit of getting into the Bible for yourself. God is the One we should follow as we obey His Word. Take a moment to pray that God will help you to be like the believers of Berea. Don't believe everything you hear, but check the Word of God out for yourself to make sure it's true. This will protect you from religion and align you to go deeper in your relationship with Jesus.

Knowing the Bible is one thing,
knowing the author is another.
~Toby Mac

DAY 7: LOOK UP! IT GETS BETTER

It's already been a week since we've been together. Starting tomorrow, I will introduce the Religious Gangsters of the New Testament, and we will begin a practical journey of how to approach some of the most common practices of the Christian life that are essential to building a relationship with God.

However, these same practices can be easily entrenched in religious mindsets that hinder relationship. More about that tomorrow. But for today, I want to encourage you that no matter what you are dealing with in your personal life, your family, or your job, it will get better. All you need to decide to do is look up.

TODAY'S WORD
Hebrews 12:2a
fixing our eyes on Jesus, the pioneer and perfecter of faith. For the joy set before him he endured the cross, scorning its shame, and sat down at the right hand of the throne of God.

WHAT DOES IT MEAN?
You may have heard of the expression to raise your head and lookup. When this expression is used in the Bible, it means getting your head off the temporal and onto the eternal. It means to stop focusing on all of the negativity surrounding your circumstances and start to have an eternal mindset. The same method was used by Jesus when He had to undergo the crucifixion. Unfortunately, negativity

and discouragement are such that you will find them whenever you want to. It lurks in both obvious and unexpected places.

Religious thoughts are fed by a temporal mindset. People who have a consistent focus on their present circumstances rather than God's plan will seek the approval of people rather than the approval of God. They focus on what they can gain now, who they can impress now, and what trials they can avoid now. The heart that focuses on relationship keeps looking to Jesus. He is the "pioneer" or "author" of our faith. In other words, He is the One who initiated our faith in Him, and He is also the One who will "perfect" or "complete" it. This means that while we're here on earth, we need to practice the most vital ingredient to please God, and that's faith. We need to trust in the One who saved us.

However, we must never forget that no trial will last forever. There will come a time when your faith will no longer have to be exercised. That time is coming when you see Jesus Christ. Once you see Him, your faith will end because you will see Him for yourself.

WHAT DOES IT MATTER?

In the meantime, we need to practice fixing our eyes on Jesus. It does not mean that we will literally see Jesus right now, but it does mean that our focus should be on the eternal rather than the temporal. Notice this is what Jesus did in His relationship with His Heavenly Father. He was able to look ahead to

the joy that would come from victory and, as a result, endure the darkest time of His existence on earth.
He was able to get through the cross because He kept His focus on God.

This is the calling that Jesus has for you today. Stop complaining, stop fighting and stop expecting the worst. God says your best days are yet to come. It takes a heart of faith that places joy in the front of uncertainty to endure times of difficulty. Your trials will tempt you to take your eyes off of Christ and focus on the temporal. But keep in mind your misguided focus will cause you to give more attention to religion than relationship.

Instead, look up and focus your eyes on Jesus. He set the example by enduring the cross because of the joy of having a close relationship with you. He was then seated on the Father's right hand. Only victorious people can sit down after a battle. The battle has been won! And He has invited you to sit with Him.

Ephesians 2:6
And God raised us up with Christ and seated us with him in the heavenly realms in Christ Jesus,
So stop stressing and sulking. It's time to get ready for more incredible blessings from God.

BEFORE YOU GO
Before you go to your next task, take a moment to pray to God that He will help you to regain your

focus. Removing your eyes off of the temporary and onto the eternal. Pray that He gives you a mindset for eternity.

When you can't see God's hand,
look up and trust His heart.

WEEK 2

AVOIDING RELIGION

DAY 8: RELIGIOUS GANGSTERS

Today, I will to introduce you to three religious gangsters and a judicial group of Jesus' time. Unfortunately, they were supposed to be the ones to lead people to Jesus, but because of their religious spirit, they were the ones who became the enemies of Christ. It's essential to mention them because they became ineffective and unproductive in their zeal for spiritual understanding. They allowed their Biblical knowledge to lead to pride and disregarded the application of the very Scriptures they were supposed to uphold.

I classify them as gangsters because they were the ones who entirely missed the heart of the law as they plotted to execute Jesus. It certainly demonstrates that Bible knowledge without a receptive heart that depends on the revelation of the Holy Spirit is not only useless but dangerous.

Let's have a quick look at these three characters today, along with the judicial group at the time of Jesus, which will lay a foundation going forward.

1. **The Pharisees** were a religious and political party at the time of Jesus. They insisted that the law of God be observed as the Scribes interpreted it.[3] When we mention the law, we usually refer to the law of Moses that was introduced in Exodus, Leviticus, and Deuteronomy. The Pharisees had a way of

adapting the meaning of the law to suit their own needs.

As a result, they went to great lengths to explain how the 613 laws found in the Old Testament should be applied, which became known as the 'tradition of the elders.'[4] Many of these traditions were not actual commands in the Scriptures, but they were treated as if they were equal to God's Word. This led to harsh legalism in which man-made rules became more important than the Bible itself.

They were quick to look down on others and were filled with pride and self-righteousness. Their hearts did not match their outward appearance as holy people. As a result, Jesus did not hold back, calling them hypocrites.

2. **The Scribes** were members of a professional class of people who studied the Old Testament Scriptures and served as copyists, editors, and teachers. Before their popularity, the priests were responsible for the Old Testament Scriptures' scientific study and professional communication.

However, this role was eventually passed on to the Scribes. "Their official interpretation of the meaning of the Law eventually became more important than the Law itself."[5] By Jesus' time, the Scribes were a new upper class among the Jewish people. They became filled with pride, like the Pharisees, and Jesus boldly rebuked them for their hypocrisy as well.

3. **The Sadducees** were the third group in Jesus' time. This Jewish faction also opposed Jesus during His ministry. They are mainly known for their denial of the bodily resurrection. The high priests and the most influential priesthood members mainly were Sadducees, as we see in the book of Acts.

   Acts 5:17
   Then the high priest and all his associates, who were members of the party of the Sadducees, were filled with jealousy.

   It is important to note that the Sadducees rejected "the tradition of the elders" that the Pharisees upheld. They also felt that the Scribes should not be the ones to interpret the law but themselves as Sadducees and priests. They did not believe in rewards or punishments after death, heaven or hell, nor angels or spirits.[6] They were the ones who opposed Jesus and played a major role in His arrest and preliminary hearing. They were the ones, along with others, who urged Pilate to crucify Jesus.

4. At this time, it's important to mention a judicial group called **the Sanhedrin.** The word means "a council or assembly." They were the highest ruling body and court of justice among the Jewish people in the time

of Jesus. It was led by the high priest, who would most likely be a Sadducee. They served as the supreme court of the Jews. The Romans denied the power of capital punishment to the Sanhedrin. This is why the Jews told Pilate that it was not lawful for them to put anyone to death. John 18:31.

Although the Sadducees made up the majority of the composition of the Sanhedrin, the Pharisees also managed to have a significant influence on the ruling council based on their popularity. For the most part, the Sadducees and Pharisees did not get along. It's essential to note that opposing forces would unite, even if it's temporary, when they identify a common enemy. In this case, the common enemy was Jesus Christ. They formed an alliance against the King of the Jews to ensure that His crucifixion would be executed.

Mark 15:1
Very early in the morning, the chief priests, with the elders, the teachers of the law and the whole Sanhedrin, made their plans. So they bound Jesus, led him away and handed him over to Pilate.

Before Jesus went to the cross, He gave us dire warnings about the negative influence of these religious parties. This is because religion stifles relationship.

WHAT DOES IT MATTER?

Our remaining time together in this devotional will expose the hearts of this religious crew. We must learn the warning lessons Jesus gave us so that we avoid becoming like them. At the same time, we will expound on the counter teachings of Jesus, which are designed to foster and maintain a close relationship with God. Some of these teachings are so simple that we tend to miss them. And yet so powerful that if we applied them, it would transform our Christian experience, forging a dynamic relationship with God.

BEFORE YOU GO

We all tend to lead busy lives, but we can never be too busy to pray. Before going on to your next thing, take some time to pray and ask God to open your heart to what we will discover from tomorrow and beyond. God wants you to experience a genuine, heart-felt relationship with Him. You won't regret it.

When you're too religious, you tend to point your finger to judge instead of extending your hand to help.
~ Steve Maraboli

DAY 9: DO WHAT THEY SAY

We cannot explore the reality of being religious without looking at some highlights from Matthew 23. This passage is so significant that some have called it the scathing denunciation of false religion. It is the falsehood that tries to present itself on the stage of life under the guise of truth. This passage is quite significant because it reveals the fact that Jesus hates religion. After all, He knows the eternal damage it can cause in the lives of its followers.

This chapter is Jesus' last public message delivered to the crowds.[7] It was given on the Tuesday of passion week, the week that Jesus would die. It comes at the end of His earthly ministry as a striking warning for all who decide to come to God. As we've seen, the only way to enter a relationship with God is by His grace in a genuine relationship based on the person and work of Christ. It's the only way one can be given Christ's righteousness as a gift. Salvation cannot be earned based on your good works. Such good works are steeped in self-righteousness like the Pharisees and the teachers of the law.

TODAY'S WORD
Matthew 23:1-4
Then Jesus said to the crowds and to his disciples: 2 "The teachers of the law and the Pharisees sit in Moses' seat. 3 So you must be careful to do everything they tell you. But do not do what they do, for they do not practice what

they preach. ⁴ They tie up heavy, cumbersome loads and put them on other people's shoulders, but they themselves are not willing to lift a finger to move them.

WHAT DOES IT MEAN?

The teachers of the law were the Jewish scholars of Jesus' day. Usually made up of the Scribes who interpreted the law. The Pharisees favored the Scribes' interpretation of the law rather than the Sadducees. These are the ones that sit in Moses' seat.

Moses' seat was considered to be a position of authority. In other words, they thought themselves to be the authorized successors of Moses as teachers of the law of God.[8] It's interesting to note that the literal translation for Matthew 23:2 is "The Scribes and Pharisees have seated themselves in Moses seat."[9] Apparently, the synagogues had an official chair called "Moses' seat."[10] It was common in Jesus' time for the teacher of the day to sit and expound on the interpretation of the law, which is what is referred to by Jesus here.

However, notice Jesus says to listen and obey what they say, but do not do what they tell you because they don't practice what they preach. A religious person will be careful to appear holy on the outside but has a heart that is far from God. They end up putting a heavy load on the shoulders of those who come to God because when you attempt to give out the truth without grace, you end up committing brutality. They were good at beating people up with the Word of God but lacked the heart to teach with the actual authority of God. A lack of grace in the pulpit leads to a heavy burden in the pew. Likewise, graceless teaching in any church will lead to legalistic, judgmental people in the congregation. It's the result of self-centered leaders that place burdens on others but refuse to help them carry the heavy load they created.

WHAT DOES IT MATTER?

If you are receiving from teachers who do not practice what they preach, it's best to find another teacher. It's vitally important that you listen to those who point you to the grace of God. If not, you'll experience an increased burden.

God wants you to be a man or woman of God who hears His Word and puts it into practice as you share it with others. In the Christian life, you don't want to say, "Do what I say and not what I do." Instead, you can declare, "Let's do what God is calling us to do together."

BEFORE YOU GO

Please take a moment to pray to God and ask Him to ensure that you not only hear the Word, but do it. In this short life, seek to put God's Word in your everyday practice. You will become a magnet in which people who sincerely desire to grow will seek to be encouraged by your words.

It doesn't matter if you can quote the Bible,
if you live like you've never opened it.
~ David Campbell

DAY 10: LOOK AT ME

The greatest problem that religion fosters is the desire for recognition and approval from others. Thus, religion has as its central theme the praise of people rather than the praise of God. Jesus made this clear in the passage we're going to look at today.

TODAY'S WORD
Matthew 23:5-7
5 "Everything they do is done for people to see: They make their phylacteries wide and the tassels on their garments long; 6 they love the place of honor at banquets and the most important seats in the synagogues; 7 they love to be greeted with respect in the marketplaces and to be called 'Rabbi' by others.

WHAT DOES IT MEAN?
Jesus exposes the motives behind the good works of the teachers of the law to a gathered crowd and His disciples. All the good works they carry out is to be seen by others to impress them. They love to appear holy even by the dress they've selected. Jesus said they make their phylacteries wide.

What are Phylacteries?
It was a practice in which Jews would place Scripture passages onto separate strips of parchment paper and place them in two small leather boxes. There would be leather straps attached to the boxes so they could strap the boxes

to be held in place on their foreheads and left arm during their morning prayers. The practice may have originated after the Jews were exiled to Babylon as some decided to take Moses' instructions literally, as in the book of Deuteronomy.

Deuteronomy 6:6, 8
[6] These commandments that I give you today are to be on your hearts. [8] Tie them as symbols on your hands and bind them on your foreheads.

Photographs showing how the phylactery is worn [11]

It was a practice at the time of Jesus, which is still carried out today by Orthodox Jews. However, the teachers of the law of Jesus' time made their straps extra wide for the sole purpose of being noticed by others.

The other modification they made to their garments was the tassels. Moses introduced these tassels in the Old Testament.

Numbers 15:38
"Speak to the Israelites and say to them:
'Throughout the generations to come you are to
make tassels on the corners of your garments,
with a blue cord on each tassel.

They were "reminder" tassels.

Numbers 15:39
You will have these tassels to look at and so you
will remember all the commands of the Lord, that
you may obey them and not prostitute yourselves
by chasing after the lusts of your own hearts and
eyes.

However, the religious leaders made their tassels
extra-long to be noticed by others.

They also loved positions with seats of prominence
along with titles of honor such as "Rabbi," which
means "my great one." It was a title that Jesus later
forbade the disciples to use.

WHAT DOES IT MATTER?
What a rebuke even for our time! It's a reminder
that we need to be sensitive to our motives
regarding anything we do for God. Do you pray, lead
a ministry, sing on the worship team, or sing in a
choir, to be recognized by others? If so, you are on
the road to becoming a religious person.
Jesus' teaching is also a sobering thought for
Christian leaders today who enjoy seats of
prominence and self-appointed titles. Some leaders

get offended because you address them as Pastor when they feel it should be Bishop, even though the terms were used synonymously in the Bible. Pastor refers to the gift and Bishop the office.

Bigger and fancier seats and long titles make no impression on Jesus at all. He's always looking for servant leadership. He evaluates every leader and layperson's heart and takes more notice of what you do outside of public recognition.

BEFORE YOU GO
Today we need to take the time to pray and ask God to reveal anything that we do for the credit of others. Also, ask Him for the grace to change so that the primary audience we seek to please is God Himself.

A person's character is shown through their actions in life, not where they sit on Sunday.
~Navonne Johns

ᕲᗩY 11: THᕮ ᗷIG 3

Today we are going to look at another rebuke Jesus brought to the Scribes and the Pharisees.

TODAY'S WORD
Matthew 23:23-24
²³ "Woe to you, teachers of the law and Pharisees, you hypocrites! You give a tenth of your spices—mint, dill and cumin. But you have neglected the more important matters of the law—justice, mercy and faithfulness. You should have practiced the latter, without neglecting the former. ²⁴ You blind guides! You strain out a gnat but swallow a camel.

WHAT DOES IT MEAN?
One thing that the teachers of the law knew how to do was tithe. They prided themselves in the whole process of giving a tenth of whatever they had to God. In this matter, they demonstrated significant priority to the small things but neglected the big things. It is the hallmark for falling into the rut of being religious.

Indeed the Old Testament law required tithing. In the New Testament, Jesus continually lifted the standard of giving because of all He has given us in Christ. He was not condemning giving but was condemning the use of tithing to conceal the Big 3 elements that matter most. The Big 3 are justice, mercy, and faithfulness.

The Pharisees and teachers of the law broke down tithing right to the spices in their kitchen. Jesus mentions the smallest spices from plants: mint, dill, and cumin. While meticulously following the law in the area of tithing, they neglected to manifest the fruit of transformation.[12] According to the Jews, a fly and a camel were considered unclean. So that's why Jesus said you strain out a fly but eat a camel! What a word picture!

Let's look at the Big 3 that Jesus mentions:

JUSTICE
Justice has the idea of doing what is right for those who could not defend themselves or were bullied by others. In Jesus' day, people would invoke false condemnation by being a false witness, resulting in a lack of justice for the individual. This practice was especially true for orphans and widows. They did not stand for the cause of the innocent and unprotected. Instead of coming by their side, they would contribute to the unwarranted condemnation.

MERCY
Mercy has been described as not getting the punishment that you deserve. God made it clear that only those who have genuinely received grace and mercy can give it to others. James, the half-brother of Jesus, promised that judgment without mercy will be given to anyone who is not merciful.

He reminded us that *"...Mercy triumphs over judgment." (James 2:13b).*

FAITHFULNESS
Faithfulness means more than being reliable. It bears the idea of being faithful or true to what you believe about God. It simply means that your life supports what you profess to believe. It does not equate to perfection but a sense of genuineness before God to follow Jesus in obedience.

WHAT DOES IT MATTER
As you reflect on your own life, think about how you measure up to the Big 3:

Justice: Do you seek to help those who don't have a voice or are opposed by others?

Mercy: Are you able to forgive and withhold from others what they may rightly deserve? For if you show mercy, God will show mercy to you when you need it.

Faithfulness: Are you one who seeks to obey God in private rather than appear to obey God in public? Then you are on the road to a growing relationship with Christ. God wants you to "live out" rather than "leave out" Who it is that you profess to serve. It's not about just showing up, but it's about fulfilling the calling that Jesus has on your life.

BEFORE YOU GO

Before moving on, take the time to do what matters most. Go to the throne of grace to ask God to make these three areas prominent in your personal life. Uphold justice, show mercy, and live out faithfulness.

The prophet Micah put it this way:
Micah 6:8
He has shown you, O mortal, what is good. And what does the LORD require of you? To act justly and to love mercy and to walk humbly with your God.

Humility is not thinking less of yourself,
It's thinking of yourself less.
~ C.S. Lewis

DAY 12: A BAD INFLUENCE

You may recall growing up, and your mother or father would at times caution you about the people you hang around or who you choose as your friends. Well, Jesus is doing the same thing in this passage with God's children. He warns them sharply about how the self-righteous teachers of the law and Pharisees would have a bad influence on the lives of their hearers.

TODAY'S WORD
Mathew 23:13,15
13 "Woe to you, teachers of the law and Pharisees, you hypocrites! You shut the door of the kingdom of heaven in people's faces. You yourselves do not enter, nor will you let those enter who are trying to.
15 "Woe to you, teachers of the law and Pharisees, you hypocrites! You travel over land and sea to win a single convert, and when you have succeeded, you make them twice as much a child of hell as you are.

WHAT DOES IT MEAN?
What a scathing rebuke! Jesus is not mincing any words, is He? What a vivid description of how much God hates religion because of what religion produces. Do you realize that religion gives people a false sense of spiritual security and comfort while cradling them to hell? Religion cuts off people from experiencing true life, which is life eternal. Someone who promotes religion over relationship

may not possess eternal life themselves and at the same time prevents others from obtaining it for themselves.

In addition, Jesus states they go out of their way to win a single convert to Judaism, but because of their controlling influence over those they reach, their converts are even worse off! Jesus uses strong words here. He describes them as becoming 'twice as much as a child of hell' as their teachers! Jesus is teaching that anyone who promotes religion over relationship has the propensity to reproduce the same religious spirit in the lives of their students.

WHAT DOES IT MATTER?
Churches with graceless legalistic leaders will only duplicate the same ruthless spirit in their followers. It's certainly a warning to ensure that we don't allow manufactured rules, pride, or the quest for a position in the church to short circuit the flow of the grace of God in our lives.

BEFORE YOU GO
Before leaving to the next activity, take the time to pray and ask God to reveal any area in your life where you allow the teaching of others to influence you. Also, pray that you are not influencing others towards religion rather than a sincere relationship with Christ.

A good leader takes care of those in their charge. A bad leader takes charge of those in their care.
~ Simon Sinek

DAY 13: FROM THE INSIDE-OUT

The greatest mistake that the Scribes and Pharisees made was to focus more on what they looked like on the outside than who they were on the inside. The applause of others was more important than the acceptance of God.

Let's look at today's passage.

TODAY'S WORD
Matthew 23:25-28

25 "Woe to you, teachers of the law and Pharisees, you hypocrites! You clean the outside of the cup and dish, but inside they are full of greed and self-indulgence. 26 Blind Pharisee! First, clean the inside of the cup and dish, and then the outside also will be clean. 27 "Woe to you, teachers of the law and Pharisees, you hypocrites! You are like whitewashed tombs, which look beautiful on the outside but on the inside are full of the bones of the dead and everything unclean. 28 In the same way, on the outside you appear to people as righteous but on the inside you are full of hypocrisy and wickedness.

WHAT DOES IT MEAN?

The teachers of the law were excellent at manifesting their own self-righteousness. They made sure that their religious ceremonies were conducted with pomp and circumstance. They put great effort into the wrong areas and neglected the core issues of the heart.

Their real issue was greed and self-indulgence. They were never satisfied! They always wanted more. In addition, they did not deny themselves the things they shouldn't have. They managed to look good on the outside while fulfilling their sinful desire on the inside.

It is for this reason Jesus elaborates that they are just like whitewashed tombs. The exterior looked beautiful and clean, but the interior was full of dead bones and decay. A person in Jesus' time who stepped on a grave would become ceremonially unclean. This was based on the Old Testament law.

Numbers 19:16
"Anyone out in the open who touches someone who has been killed with a sword or someone who has died a natural death, or anyone who touches a human bone or a grave, will be unclean for seven days.

Many of the graveyards in Bermuda and other countries are whitewashed to look good. However, the Jewish people took the time to whitewash their tombs as well for a different reason. They did it so that they would be easily visible to avoid them, especially at night.

Jesus likened religious people to a gravesite. They looked good on the outside in front of people, but were full of decay on the inside in front of God.

WHAT DOES IT MATTER?

The signs of the end times are that greed and self-indulgence would rule people. It's the same 'grave' mistake that the religious in Jesus' time made. We need to be sensitive to the Holy Spirit to ensure we're not like them. It's important to note that greed is subtle. It's the greedy person who is least likely to see the state of their own heart.

As believers, the other warning for us is we need to be aware when our hearts gravitate to more and more material things. If you find your heart constantly desiring the best of everything, such as the best phone, the best computer, the best clothes or shoes, that could very well be greed. Greed is more like the slow leak of a tire. It gradually builds to the point you feel you won't be happy without certain "things". You conclude that you would be miserable without that which is 'new and improved.' It's no wonder when Jesus was on earth, He constantly warned about the deception of riches.

BEFORE YOU GO

Today's prayer will be about material things. Take the time to pray for God's protection against your heart falling in love with things more than people and in self-indulgence more than God.

He is no fool who gives what he cannot keep
to gain what he cannot lose.
~ Jim Elliott

DAY 14: THERE'S HOPE

We only have one week left together. I am delighted that you are continuing to get into God's Word through this devotional. Before we undergo the final seven days, I want to encourage you with the hope that Jesus provided even in His direct rebuke to the religious leaders.

The religious leaders may have started their spiritual journey with good motives to please God. After all, they had a zeal for spiritual matters, tended to be hardworking, and were loyal to their system of righteousness. However, their rules, regulations, and pride blinded them from experiencing direct contact with God and His grace.

Even though Jesus condemned them for creating their form of righteousness, you can still hear the compassion of Jesus leaking through His fearless rebuke in Matthew 23. Jesus concludes His discourse in today's passage.

Matthew 23:37-39
37 "Jerusalem, Jerusalem, you who kill the prophets and stone those sent to you, how often I have longed to gather your children together, as a hen gathers her chicks under her wings, and you were not willing. 38 Look, your house is left to you desolate. 39 For I tell you, you will not see me again until you say, 'Blessed is he who comes in the name of the Lord.'"

WHAT DOES IT MEAN?

The religious leaders were the ones who were supposed to recognize the Messiah and point the people to eternal life through the grace of God in Christ. Instead, they were the ones who were guilty of killing the prophets of God and stoning those sent to turn people to Him.

Yet, please don't miss the heart of Jesus in verse 37. He said, *"...how often I have longed to gather your children together, as a hen gathers her chicks under her wings,...".* Jesus states that He continually desired to embrace His chosen people, but they've rejected the offer. How powerful is the sin of pride that it caused them to short-change the truth for a lie?

As a result, the place of worship, which would have been the temple at this time, would be desolate. So the next time the eyes of the majority of the Jewish people would "see" Jesus would be upon His return.

WHAT DOES IT MATTER?

The heart of Jesus towards these religious people is a reminder of the hope that is in Christ. Even though there may be areas in your own life where you see religious tendencies, it is comforting to know that you serve the One who is always ready to embrace you. We need to be willing to embrace the more abundant life with a relational focus. It's encouraging to know that Jesus will turn to you whenever you desire to turn to Him.

As you've gone through this devotional, you may have had times when you discovered that you had a mindset to impress others more than God or approached your devotional or prayer life as a duty rather than a joy. There's hope! Jesus is ready to gather you to Himself.

If your Christian life has become mundane and spiritual things have become stale, there's hope. If you're tired of just surviving and "just getting through" each day, then I've got good news for you. It's your time to experience the abundant life that Jesus died for.

In our final week together, I will share the most practical principles that will take you from being religious to building a sincere relationship with Christ. You will experience a change, but only if you apply them. They are taken directly from God's Word, most of which are the words of Jesus Himself.

BEFORE YOU GO
Before we part, please pray and ask God to open your heart to the final days of Religion vs. Relationship so that you will not only desire abundance but also experience it.

In life, you don't use God to fulfill your purpose. Instead, you let God use you to fulfill His purpose.
~ Author Unknown

WEEK 3

EMBRACING RELATIONSHIP

DAY 15: GIVE BIG, RECEIVE BIG

In the final six days together, we'll look at three Christian principles that foster a close relationship with Jesus. In fact, if you're going to be a committed Christian, you need to put each of these into practice. However, just doing it isn't good enough. These practices must be done with the right heart and motive. Each must be carried out in the right way. The first of these spiritual disciplines have to do with giving.

Jesus introduced the importance of giving in the context of rewards.

TODAY'S WORD
Matthew 6:1
"Be careful not to practice your righteousness in front of others to be seen by them. If you do, you will have no reward from your Father in heaven.

WHAT DOES IT MEAN?
Jesus clarifies that we shouldn't practice our righteousness in front of people to be recognized by them. Practicing righteousness means the good deeds we claim to do for God. Once again, we see how it's not just about doing what's right. It's also about the motive behind it. Whenever we do something to be noticed by others, no matter how sacrificial it is, we forfeit God's reward for man's reward. This brings us to the doctrine of rewards. **Did you know God has placed an incentive rewards program right into the Christian life?**

Some Christians struggle because God wants to reward them for doing good, but the Bible clearly teaches it. First of all, it's important to note that eternal life is never a reward because you can't earn it. Instead, eternal life is a gift given when one admits they have sinned and believes that Jesus died on the cross and rose again for their sins. You can never earn salvation. It's a gift given by God's grace through your faith in Jesus.

Rewards, however, can be earned and should be earned because it's God's will. Whenever you do anything for God as a believer, with the right motive to be seen by God and not people, God has promised to reward you.

WHAT DOES IT MATTER?

People focused on the temporary will only see the benefit of obtaining the praise they get from people. So they make it known to others the good things they do for the church or the less fortunate. However, people focused on the eternal are only concerned about giving before God and don't announce the good they do for others. They would rather receive God's reward. After all, God's rewards come in various forms in this life and in the life to come.

God is not limited as to how He wants to reward you. For example, if someone gives a donation to the church, it doesn't always mean that their reward is limited to finances. It could come in the form of healing, family blessings, protection, and exceptional business deals, or other material or spiritual things. The ways of how God rewards us are limitless. The bottom line is that you can never out-give God. He has promised that whatever you do for Him, even if it is giving a cup of cold water to one in need, will be rewarded (Matthew 10:42). Rewarding us for doing good is always on Jesus' mind. We only need to look at His last words in the book of Revelation in chapter 22, verse 12.

Revelation 22:12
"Look, I am coming soon! My reward is with me, and I will give to each person according to what they have done.

Jesus can't wait to reward you for all that you do for Him. You may struggle with that thought and think, 'but I shouldn't give to be rewarded;' however, Jesus thinks otherwise. He wants you to look forward to being rewarded so much that He placed in the Bible various rewards you can earn.

Here are some examples:

First of all, there are the crowns Jesus can't wait to give you. The Bible describes at least five of them:

1. **The Incorruptible Crown** for self-discipline for saying no to sin and living for Jesus - 1 Corinthians 9:24,25.

2. **The Crown of Rejoicing** for investing in growth and discipleship of others -

1 Thessalonians 2:19.

3. **The Crown of Righteousness** for longing for Jesus Christ to come back - 2 Timothy 4:8.

4. **The Crown of Life** for those who persevere in the most challenging trials - James 1:12.

5. **The Crown of Glory** for pastors and elders that serve people as servant leaders - 1 Peter 5:4.

The rewards that God gives are not limited to these crowns. Rewards are given for almost anything that you decide to do for Jesus to please Him rather than people. Here is a non-exhaustive list of some of the rewards God is looking forward to giving you.

God wants to reward you:
- *When you work hard at your place of employment - Colossians 3:23-24.*
- *When you are faithful in trials - 1 Peter 1:6-7.*
- *When you are careful not to be deceived - 2 John 1:7-8.*
- *When you pray and fast - Matthew 6:6, 18.*
- *When you help those who are hungry, imprisoned, or unclothed – Matthew 25:37-40.*
- *When you don't retaliate when people insult you and falsely accuse you – Luke 6:22,23*
- *When you love your enemies and do good to them – Luke 6:35.*
- *When you give generously financially – Luke 6:38.*

- *When you help people who cannot return the favor – Luke 4:12-14.*[13]

BEFORE YOU GO

Have a look at the above list again. You can see how rewards are significant to God. He even rewards us for what we can only do with His power. How amazing is that! Today, please take the time to thank Him for being a God that is so generous that He wants to reward us for simply doing what we should do in and for Christ.

Our rewards in heaven are a result of God's crowning His own gifts.
~ *Saint Augustine*

ĐAY 16: HOW TO GIVE

The whole aspect of giving has always been a hot topic in Christian circles, and it was a hot topic for Jesus. In fact, giving was so important to Jesus that he emphasized it in His teaching. Approximately 16 of the 38 parables were concerned with how to handle money and possessions.[14] It's a vital topic because material things are the number one distraction from spiritual things in affluent countries. So, let's discover how the religious-driven people versus relationship-driven people give to God.

Matthew 6:1-4
[1] "Be careful not to practice your righteousness in front of others to be seen by them. If you do, you will have no reward from your Father in heaven.
[2] "So when you give to the needy, do not announce it with trumpets, as the hypocrites do in the synagogues and on the streets, to be honored by others. Truly I tell you, they have received their reward in full.
[3] But when you give to the needy, do not let your left hand know what your right hand is doing, [4] so that your giving may be in secret. Then your Father, who sees what is done in secret, will reward you.

WHAT DOES IT MEAN?
Those who are bound by religion can't help but give to be noticed. They give to a need, even in the church, because they want people to think they are

generous and good people. The notice they get from others becomes their sole reward. God has decided He won't acknowledge it because the giving was done with the wrong motive.

He then describes how the Pharisees gave. The classic title that Jesus gave the Pharisees and teachers of the law was 'hypocrites.' There were three primary practices that the Pharisees would pride themselves on. It was giving, praying, and fasting. Now each of these are necessary to be a growing and maturing Christian, but they have to be practiced in the right way.

The Pharisees did them to try and earn salvation and to get the praises of people. The catastrophic problem with that is they would obtain the temporary glory of people and miss out on eternal life because salvation can't be earned. So whenever we give to impress others, we come up as three-fold losers. We may get praise from people, but it won't last, then we miss out on the blessing of rewards that God wants to give us. Finally, we miss out on bringing glory to God.

WHAT DOES IT MATTER?

It's tempting to do things for people's praise simply because of our own insecurity. It builds up our ego, but it doesn't pay. The key to failure is to try and please people. The trumpets in the passage appear to be figurative and describe how much the giver tells others of their giving. However, when you want to build a relationship with Jesus, it is enough to know that God sees it and will bless you accordingly.

Jesus continues to expound on this topic by stating, don't let your left hand know what your right hand is doing. This was a proverbial saying during the first century that means, keep it on the 'down-low.' There is no need to announce your good works to others to be noticed when it comes to financial giving.

When you want to bless someone, keep it between yourself and the recipient. There is no need to tell others what you did because if you do… that's the only reward you will get. People want the praise of others because they have no idea of the amazing rewards that God can give if we simply obey Him in this area.

Don't fall into the trap of being religious like the Pharisees who give for man. Make sure that when you give, you give for God.

BEFORE YOU GO
Giving is an essential practice to grow in Christ. Giving of your tithes and offerings is what you should do, but make sure you provide it for the glory of God. Take the time to pray to God and ask Him for the right heart as you give. Ask Him to stop you in your tracks when you find yourself bragging about what you did for someone else. And you will be rewarded by God on a level whereby you won't be disappointed.

When God blesses you financially,
don't raise your standard of living.
Raise your standard of giving.
~ *Mark Batterson*

DAY 17: BEHIND CLOSED DOORS

The second foundational practice in the Christian life is prayer. Prayer is not limited to Christians. People from all over the world pray to various gods and deities. Yet, the Bible clearly reveals that there is One true God, and the only way to access Him is through the person and work of Jesus Christ on the cross.

Hebrews 10:19-20
19 Therefore, brothers and sisters, since we have confidence to enter the Most Holy Place by the blood of Jesus, 20 by a new and living way opened for us through the curtain, that is, his body,

When one believes in the death and resurrection of Christ, we are given direct 24/7 access to the throne of Grace. We know we should pray, but we're seldom taught how to do it. When Jesus came to earth, He revealed what prayer should look like. He gave us broad guidelines so that our communion with God would be most effective and relational rather than a mundane religious exercise. Let's look at it together.

TODAY'S WORD
Matthew 6:5-6
5 "And when you pray, do not be like the hypocrites, for they love to pray standing in the synagogues and on the street corners to be seen by others. Truly I tell you, they have received their reward in full. 6 But when you pray, go into

your room, close the door and pray to your Father, who is unseen. Then your Father, who sees what is done in secret, will reward you.

WHAT DOES IT MEAN?
Jesus made it clear that there's a drastic difference between religious prayer and relational prayer. His primary teaching is 'why you pray' determines 'how you pray.' Jesus said when you pray, don't be like the hypocrites, the religious gangsters we talked about on Day 8. They love to use prayer as a means to look 'holy.' They enjoy it when people hear them pray because they gain a greater satisfaction of broadcasting their prayers in the ears of people than in the ears of God.

As a result, God does not hear their prayers. Their prayers are not answered by God. The only reward they will obtain is a sense of pride because their hearers thought the prayers were so amazing. What a waste of time!

WHAT DOES IT MATTER?
Jesus then gives us a specific practice to undertake if we want to build an authentic relationship with God. You see, prayer's purpose is to build relationship. It's communication. Like any marriage, friendship, and family, the relationship will deepen if there is healthy communication. Without open communication, the relationship will be strained.

Many may recall the time that they were dating. Remember when you could talk for hours, and it would seem like minutes? Why? Because you were building a relationship, and you loved doing it.

Unfortunately, time has a way of leading us to take those closest to us for granted, and the wonder of the relationship can be lost and needs to be revived. Maybe because we think they will always be with us. However, there is a God in heaven that has never lost the wonder of spending time with you. In fact, He can't wait until you make the time. So much so that Jesus commands us to go into a room, close the door, and pray to God one-on-one.

It is for this reason Jesus says to go into a room. This is referring to a designated place that you have to pray. The room Jesus is referring to is most likely the Greek word used for "storeroom" because it had a door that you could close, unlike most rooms in first-century houses.[15]

Jesus is not against public prayer with others because we are also commanded to do so. However, to build a personal relationship with God, you need to do that alone. Let me try and illustrate. Let's go back to dating. If you were dating someone and wanted to get to know them, but that person always brought a third party on your dates, how would you feel? At first, you may tolerate it and even enjoy meeting the additional person. But after a short while, you will get frustrated because you want to get to know the person you're interested in alone. Why? Because the entire dynamic changes; it is more focused, more meaningful, and necessary to get to know the person well. One-on-one communication is imperative to build a close relationship. The same is true with your relationship with God.

There's a triple benefit when we pray to God in private. First, there is the eternal blessing of building your relationship with God. Secondly, God hears your prayers, and third, He is so thankful that you valued Him to the point of talking to Him alone, that He promised to reward you for it. So there's nothing wrong with praying in public, but it's wrong to pray in public if we're not already in the habit of praying in private.

Jesus prayed alone with the Father. In fact, there were times He sent the disciples ahead just so that He could spend time with His Father. There were other times He got up early to spend time with God.

Mark 1:35
Very early in the morning, while it was still dark, Jesus got up, left the house and went off to a solitary place, where he prayed.
You have a Father who can't wait to meet with you. He doesn't want a third party in the mix. He wants to meet you one-on-one because He loves you and values the time you spend together. Will you do it?

PUT IT INTO PRACTICE
What is going to be your designated spot to pray? _____

What is the best time for you to pray? _____

BEFORE YOU GO

Before you go, find that spot where you can go into, maybe kneel, maybe talk aloud or quietly to avoid distraction, however you feel led. Remember, there is a Creator who is waiting to meet just with you. Tomorrow we will discover the second principle that Jesus brings out on how we should pray.

If you are too busy to pray, you are busier than God wants you to be.
~ Wanda E. Brunstetter

DAY 18: HE ALREADY KNOWS

Let's face it. For many Christians, prayer brings about both the most incredible guilt and the greatest disappointment. Guilt, because we feel that we haven't been as faithful in prayer as we should. As a result, we may conclude that our prayers may not be heard or are not effective. Disappointment, because we may remember a time when we prayed for something that we really wanted, such as the healing of a spouse, family member, or loved one, that job you've been waiting so long for, or the marriage you've always dreamed about, but it didn't happen. So even the topic of prayer can come with its own baggage based on past experiences.

Although God doesn't always give us what we want, it doesn't mean that He's not all-powerful. He is. And He is also all-knowing and therefore knows what's best. This brings us to our passage for today.

TODAY'S WORD
Matthew 6:7-8
7 And when you pray, do not keep on babbling like pagans, for they think they will be heard because of their many words. 8 Do not be like them, for your Father knows what you need before you ask him.

WHAT DOES IT MEAN?
Yesterday we discovered that Jesus said we are not to pray like the hypocrites, referring to the teachers of the law and the Pharisees. Today we just read

that Jesus said we should not pray like the pagans. The term 'pagans' refers not only to unbelievers but those who pray to false gods. These worshippers used long lists of the names of their gods in their prayers. They constantly repeated their titles, hoping that by the constant babbling of their names, they would be heard and helped.[16]

As believers, Jesus is helping us understand that we can make the same grave error as we pray to the true God, that the pagans make praying to their false gods. They thought they had to use many words to be heard by their gods. We can make the same mistake. We can conclude that our prayers have to include many words or be lengthy to be more effective.

However, notice that God does not tell us how long our prayers should be. He just wants us to pray! Instead of focusing on the right formula for prayer, we should focus on developing a deeper relationship with God in prayer.

WHAT DOES IT MATTER?
This means that our number one priority shouldn't be to receive more from God. Instead, it should be to know God more. This is because the God you serve knows every detail about you. In fact, He knows more about you than you know about yourself. Therefore, He even knows about what you need before you ask Him. You are always on His mind, and He wants you to know that you are not a secondary thought. He knows, and He cares.

How do you view prayer?

Is it a list of things you want from God, such as healing, protection, and provision, or is it primarily to express your love for God and develop a deeper relationship with Him?

BEFORE YOU GO

Before you go to the next task, take some time to meditate on your prayer life. And then, realign your prayers to praise and thank God before asking Him for things. Prayer is not just about what you can get from God. Instead, it's more about getting to know the One you're talking to.

When God gives you a NO, give him a THANK YOU for He is protecting you from less than His best.
~ Author Unknown

DAY 19: TEACH ME HOW TO PRAY

The disciples in the Bible were not perfect people. They were imperfect people who had limited answers following Jesus, who had all the answers. It's no wonder they asked Jesus a fundamental question, 'How do you pray?'

Jesus answered the question with an incredible model prayer. It was not Jesus' intention that we memorize the prayer to continually recite it. Instead, it was given as a model by which we can create our own prayer to God.

However, this model gives us some significant principles to keep in mind when we talk to God. This is the way we protect ourselves from ritualism and develop a relationship with God instead.

TODAY'S WORD
Matthew 6:9-13
9 "This, then, is how you should pray:
"'Our Father in heaven, hallowed be your name,
10 your kingdom come, your will be done, on earth as it is in heaven.
11 Give us today our daily bread.
12 And forgive us our debts, as we also have forgiven our debtors.
13 And lead us not into temptation, but deliver us from the evil one.'

WHAT DOES IT MEAN?

Let's break down this prayer to better understand the example that Jesus wants us to follow. The following chart will help us to grasp the aspects that Jesus desires in our prayers. As you go through it, please consider what needs to change in your own prayer life to benefit what Jesus taught His followers.

JESUS' EXAMPLE	HOW IT MAY BE APPLIED
Our Father	As you begin, address God your Father or 'Daddy'. This is to pray relationally.
In heaven	Pray, remembering that God is all-powerful, sits on His eternal throne and in complete control.
Hallowed (or holy) is your name	As you begin your prayer, exalt His name as unique. "Holy" means "set apart."
Your kingdom come	Pray that you live out the kingdom agenda on earth.
Your will be done:	Pray for God's will to be done in every area of your life.
Give us today our daily bread	Pray, asking God for your spiritual needs every day.
Forgive us our debts as we forgive others	Ask God to show you any unnoticed sin in your life and pray for those who have mistreated or hurt you.
Lead us not into temptation	Pray that God will redirect you if you're heading into a trap of the enemy.
Deliver us from the evil one	Because evil is all around you, pray that God will protect and deliver you from the evil one and evil people.

WHAT DOES IT MATTER?

We must use this model to learn how to pray. As we stated earlier, we don't have to repeat the same prayer of Jesus. Jesus gave us the model to talk freely to God while covering the principles within it. Note that the focus of the prayer is God Himself. We must be careful to begin our prayers with exalting God for Who He is, rather than immediately treating God like Santa or a genie who fulfills our list of wants and wishes.

The focus of the prayer is that we must align ourselves with God's kingdom and His will rather than our agenda. We need to fully grasp that God's precise desires for our lives are far better than our own. His kingdom has no end, His plans are astounding, and His purposes are eternal. God can do for us immeasurably more than we can do for ourselves. For this reason, it is necessary to begin our prayers with submission to the predestined will of God.

Then we can ask for our daily provision while at the same time ensuring that we forgive the sin of others. If not, God won't forgive our sins. If you harbor unforgiveness, your prayers will bounce right off the ceiling.

Finally, we should keep in mind we are in a spiritual battle. This requires us to ask God to lead us not into the plan of the enemy but to deliver us from his evil agenda for our lives.

BEFORE YOU GO

Today, we will do something different. As you pray, continue to look at the chart above and begin to get into the practice of praying how Jesus taught you to pray. Substitute your own words as you talk to God with the outline Jesus provided. Remember, there is no such thing as a perfect prayer. Your Heavenly Daddy simply wants to spend time with you and hear your heart.

The purpose of prayer is that we get a
hold of God, not of the answer.
~ *Oswald Chambers*

DAY 20: NEGLECTED PRACTICE

As we prepare to conclude our time together. There's one other primary practice that Jesus mentions, and that is fasting. Fasting is when we deny our physical desires to create a greater focus on our spiritual needs. Fasting is so dear to God because just like we take the time to eat, we should take the time to pray. Fasting intensifies our prayers, and prayer deepens our relationship with God and intensifies our faith.

Let's look at what Jesus said about this critical practice of fasting.

TODAY'S WORD
Matthew 6:16-18
16 "When you fast, do not look somber as the hypocrites do, for they disfigure their faces to show others they are fasting. Truly I tell you, they have received their reward in full. 17 But when you fast, put oil on your head and wash your face, so that it will not be obvious to others that you are fasting, but only to your Father, who is unseen; and your Father, who sees what is done in secret, will reward you.

WHAT DOES IT MEAN?
The Scribes and teachers of the law were determined to let others know they were fasting. Why? To be considered spiritual and highly regarded. Jesus said their public recognition was the only reward they would receive.

Jesus said when you fast, don't be like them. Instead, put lotion on your head and wash your face so that people won't know you're fasting. Just like prayer, Jesus wanted fasting to be done for the right reasons and not to get the attention of others. Therefore, because you did it for God, your Father who sees what you are doing in private will reward you for it like you won't believe.

How amazing is it that the most essential and yet simple acts of growing in Christ and developing a relationship with God come with rewards from the One you're doing it for?

WHAT DOES IT MATTER?
The topic of fasting is so important but can be taken so lightly among believers. Yet fasting is so vital that the Bible records people who had some of their most incredible breakthroughs when they prayed and fasted.

Here are a few biblical examples of when to fast.

- To prepare for a new ministry ~ Mark 1:12-23.

- To seek God's will ~ Acts 14:23.

- To show grief before God ~ Nehemiah 1:1-4.

- To repent before God to obtain His mercy ~ Jonah 3:10.

- To gain victory in a battle ~ Judges 20:26.

- To worship God ~ Luke 2:37.

- To become pregnant ~ 1 Samuel 1:7.

- To experience the healing or deliverance of others ~ Matthew 17:21

BEFORE YOU GO

Before you continue on, remember that fasting is not something to be feared or to ignore. It's an uncompromising practice that you must do to grow your relationship with Christ. However, do it because of your relationship with Jesus and not to impress others or impress yourself. When it's done in secret, the rewards will be forthcoming.

Christian fasting, at its root, is the hunger of a homesickness for God.
~ *John Piper*

ÐAY 21: GROW IN GRACE

Before I go, I would like to thank God for you. You decided to get into God's Word and go deeper in your relationship with Christ. We've come to the end of this devotional, and I want to leave you with some final thoughts. Religion is the opposite of grace. You were saved by the grace of God, and you grow in that same grace. I want to leave you with this verse.

TODAY'S WORD
2 Peter 3:18
But grow in the grace and knowledge of our Lord and Savior Jesus Christ. To him be glory both now and forever! Amen.

WHAT DOES IT MEAN?
Peter made it clear that we must grow in the grace and knowledge of our Lord. Grace is not limited to salvation. It is also required for our sanctification. To go from glory to glory in your relationship with Christ, you don't need legalistic rules and religious practices. You don't even need to register for countless seminars and exhaustive Bible studies as much as you need the grace of God.

WHAT DOES IT MATTER?
The grace of God is the source of His unconditional love for us. There is nothing more powerful, enduring, and abundant as grace. God's grace contains the power to literally transform someone from the inside out. It is not an 'add-on,' it's a

necessity. You can't purchase it, work for it, or in any way position yourself to deserve it. It only comes as a free gift, and as a free gift, you can only receive it. It doesn't wait for you to change; instead, it is the source of change.

This is because grace fully understands that you cannot clean yourself no matter how hard you try. It fully grasps the fact that you can't change in your own strength. And it fully realizes that you are frail and totally weak even on your best day.

For this reason, the grace of God is only attracted to weak and humble people. When we admit our weaknesses and limitations, God comes and gives us His grace in the form of perfect strength. For this reason, God is always on standby, ready to provide you with a full dose of grace whenever you need it. It's something you can't give to others unless you've fully received it yourself.

Its purpose is to lead you into a close relationship with God that is built on His love for you so that you can have joy in sorrow, light in the darkness, perseverance in tribulations, strength in weakness, and the power to change.

It's the one thing that will protect you from religious thinking and religious practices. It will keep you from falling into the rut of the mundane. It's no wonder Paul started and ended all of his letters with grace and peace to you.

The same grace you first received when you accepted Christ, is the one essential that's required to live for Him. It's what the Spirit of God uses to fill you to experience transformative power and faith. Keep growing in the grace of God so that you will be protected from the danger of religion and continue to develop a vibrant relationship with Jesus.

BEFORE YOU GO
Thank you for being a part of Religion versus Relationship. Thank God for what He has done in your life, and ask Him to help you to recall what you've discovered in the past three weeks. Until next time, continue to grow in the grace of God.

You may not think that you're good enough,
but God's grace and love are bigger
than who you think you are.
~ Author Unknown

NOTES

[1] Barna Research Releases in Faith and Christianity. *"Most American Christians Do Not Believe that Satan and the Holy Spirit Exist."*, April 13, 2009. Accessed June 7, 2021, https://www. barna.com/research/most-american-christians-do-not-believe-that-satan-or-the-holy-spirit-exist/.

[2] Mission Bible Class. *"The Nobel Bereans"*, 2011-2021. Accessed on June 7, 2021, https://missionbibleclass.org/new-testament/part2/acts-epistle-selections/the-noble-bereans/ Access June 7, 2021.

[3] Ronald F. Youngblood, *The Nelson's Illustrative Bible Dictionary* (Oxford, England: Linn Publishing, 1985), 886.

[4] Ibid., 886.

[5] Ibid., 1030.

[6] Ibid.,1007.

[7] Warren Wiersbe, *The Bible Exposition Commentary. New Testament Volume* (Victor: Colorado Springs, Colorado, 2001), 83.

[8] *The NIV Study Bible*, 2002 Edition, Study notes (Cambridge, UK: Cambridge University Press, 2007), 1505.

[9] Warren Wiersbe, *The Bible Exposition Commentary. New Testament Volume* (Victor: Colorado Springs, Colorado, 2001), 83.

[10] *Thomas Nelson NKJV Study Bible* (Thomas Nelson Publishers: Nashville, Tennessee, 2018), 1444.

[11] Photosourced and purchased from *iStock by Getty Images*: Photo 171557081 and 1300494032. Accessed June 2021.

[12] John F. Walvoord and Roy B. Zuck, *The Bible Knowledge Commentary, New Testament Edition.* (Scripture Press Publications: Wheaton, Illinois, 1983), 42.

[13] Kevin Hallran. *"Unlocking the Bible"*, 2016. Accessed June 16, 2021, https://unlockingthebible.org/2016/08 /10-things-christ-promises-to-reward/.

[14] Christianity Today. *"Statistic: Jesus' Teaching on Money"*, 2021. Accessed June 15, 2021, https://www.preaching today.com/ illustrations/1996/december/410.html.

[15] *The NIV Study Bible*, 2002 Edition, Study notes (Cambridge, UK: Cambridge University Press, 2007), 1478.

[16] Ibid., 1478.

ABOUT THE AUTHORS

Gary and Belle Simons are founders of **Reveal International**, a teaching ministry dedicated to leadership development, training church planters, and the spiritual growth of Christians. Gary is a high honors graduate of Word of Life Bible Institute, New York, with Diplomas in Bible, Youth Ministry, Missions, and Evangelism. He also earned an Undergraduate Degree in Biblical Studies and a Graduate Degree in Counseling from Carin University Graduate School, Pennsylvania. He then obtained a Graduate Certificate in Historical and Geographical Settings of the Bible from Jerusalem University College, Israel. His biblical teaching gift has been a blessing to churches and ministries worldwide in North, Central, and South America, Africa, Europe, Asia, and the Far East.

Belle earned an Undergraduate Degree in Food Science from Tunghai University, Taichung, Taiwan, before God called her to missions. She has served as a missionary for Operation Mobilization, fulfilling various administrative roles before joining the Ministry Preparation Team. This involved networking and planning with governments and church leaders to assess and fulfill diverse spiritual and societal needs. She has also been involved in various Mandarin Chinese translation ministry projects, including assisting author Dr. Wright Doyle's work on the Chinese-Greek Lexicon of the New Testament. Belle has recently served as a lead translator for World Teach, Southeast Asia that will open the door for the Chinese-speaking world to go deeper into the Word of God.

Gary and Belle regularly minister between Bermuda, Taiwan, Ethiopia, Kenya, and Myanmar while training hundreds of church planting pastors each year with Petros Network. Between them, they have conducted cross-cultural ministry in over 50 countries. They minister as servant-leaders of GracePoint in Bermuda with an incredible leadership team. They also serve as Country Coordinators for Walk Thru the Bible Taiwan. Recently they have been appointed as the Overseers of the Masai Tribe Churches of the Masai Mara, Kenya. Gary and Belle are happily married and have three children, Aiden, Jasmine, and Arian.

THE SHOCKING TEACHINGS OF JESUS

This 14-Day devotional will both encourage and challenge you. When we're face to face with the shocking teachings of Jesus, it's as if He draws a clearly defined line in the sand. We can decide to either continue in our way of living or cross over to the abundant life by making some drastic changes. His teachings help us realize that maintaining the status quo as a Christian is no longer acceptable because Christ calls us to a deeper walk.

RESCUE: *Character Study of Moses*

As we present what really happened in Moses' life directly from the Bible, you'll find that although he lived over 3,000 years ago, His life lessons will become your own. The relative truth from this Bible character will jump right off the pages and directly into your heart. His successes and failures, along with the challenges in between, will transform how you see yourself, your problems, your inadequacies, and most importantly, your God.

Made in the USA
Las Vegas, NV
02 May 2024